VALENTINE FUN

Activity Book

by Judith Stamper

Illustrated by Bari Weissman and T. R. Garcia

Troll

METRIC EQUIVALENTS

1 inch = 2.54 centimeters
1 square inch = 6.45 square centimeters
1 foot = 30.5 centimeters

1 teaspoon = 5 milliliters (approx.)
1 tablespoon = 15 milliliters (approx.)
1 fluid ounce = 29.6 milliliters
1 cup = .24 liter
1 pint = .47 liter
1 quart = .95 liter
1 pound = .45 kilogram

Conversion from Fahrenheit to Celsius:
subtract 32 and then multiply the
remainder by 5/9

Contents

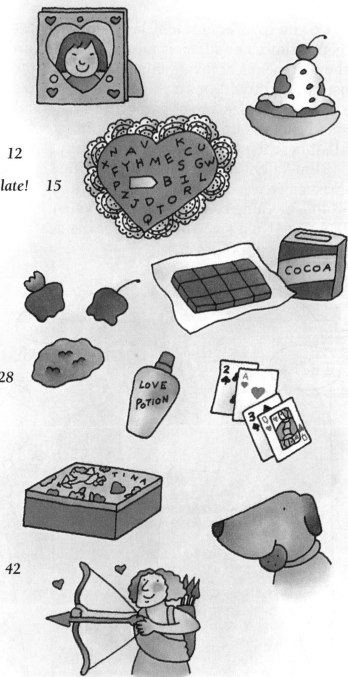

Introduction

Do you love Valentine's Day? This celebration of friendship and love is a happy time. For some, it means sending cards to special friends. For others, it means enjoying chocolate and other tasty treats. The many customs and traditions of Valentine's Day give us a holiday filled with fun.

How did Valentine's Day begin? This holiday is so ancient that its exact history is unclear. But we do know some legends about Saint Valentine, the person for whom this day is named.

Saint Valentine lived in Rome about 1700 years ago, at the time when Christianity was a new religion. The Roman emperor of the time had forbidden young soldiers to marry. Valentine, a priest, secretly married the men to their sweethearts. After his death, Valentine became known as the patron saint of lovers.

An even older custom connected to Valentine's Day is the Roman holiday called Lupercalia. This festival was celebrated close to the present date of Valentine's Day, February 14th. Over the years, the Lupercalia festival became a romantic holiday. Young Roman men and women drew names from a jar to find out who their sweethearts might be during the coming year.

As centuries passed, the traditions of the Lupercalia mixed with the legends of Saint Valentine. The holiday spread through Europe and then to North America. It became a custom for friends to exchange cards and boxes of candy. Valentine's Day became a time for showing love and friendship.

This book has crafts, recipes, jokes, games, and facts — all about Valentine's Day and its customs. Some are traditions from the past. Others are up-to-date, fun-filled ideas to make this Valentine's Day your best ever.

Picture This

One picture is worth a thousand words. Now picture this — a framed photo of your sweetheart. Here's something to help you remember your valentine.

Materials

Colored mat board (one with opening; one without)
Scissors
Paint (dimensional, tempera, or acrylic)
Paintbrushes
Tape or glue
Packages of accessories such as glitter or stones

Steps

1. Using the mat board with opening, cut the opening into a heart shape.

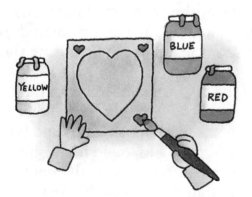

2. Paint a design around the heart-shaped opening on the board.

3. Add glitter, stones, or other decorations by setting into dimensional paint before it dries. If using other paint, allow to dry before adding decorations with glue.

4. Apply glue or two-sided tape to the back of the uncut mat board along three edges as shown.

5. Press back side of decorated frame onto glue or tape. Let dry.

6. Slide photo or drawing of your sweetheart into frame. You may want to add an extra piece of tape at the bottom to help keep the frame tight.

6A.

6B.

7. If you wish, you may glue or tape a frame stand to back of frame.

7A.

7B.

Broken Hearts

Some valentines are sweet and frilly. But these valentines are tricky and fun! Be a heartbreaker this year. Puzzle your friends by sending broken-heart valentines.

Materials

Red poster board or heavy construction paper
Markers or crayons
Pencil

Scissors
Envelope
Ruler

Steps

1. On red poster board or construction paper, draw a large heart, about eight inches wide at its widest point. Cut it out with scissors.

2. Write a funny message on the front of the heart with a marker or crayon. Here are some messages that you can use — or make up some of your own.

YOU CRACK ME UP.
YOU MAKE ME GO TO PIECES.
YOU GIVE ME A HEART ATTACK.
I'M LOVESICK OVER YOU.

3. Decorate the edges of the heart with markers or crayons. Then sign your name.

4. Turn the heart over and draw lines on the back with a pencil. Make the lines look like a jigsaw puzzle, drawing about 15 puzzle pieces.

5. Cut the heart into pieces along the lines you've drawn. (Make sure to cut your name into two or more pieces to make the puzzle even more mysterious.)

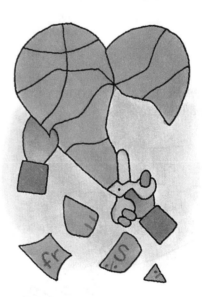

6. Put the pieces of your "broken heart" into an envelope and send them to a friend. He or she will have fun putting your valentine puzzle together.

I ♥ Ice Cream

If you love ice cream, Valentine's Day is the perfect time to show it. Think of the terrific treats you can make with ice cream and toppings in valentine colors of red and white. Add the official candy of Valentine's Day — chocolate — to make a dessert that you'll fall in love with.

Valentine Float

You Will Need

Vanilla ice cream   Ice-cream scoop
Strawberry soda   Straw
Tall glass   Small spoon

Steps

1. Put three scoops of vanilla ice cream in a tall glass.

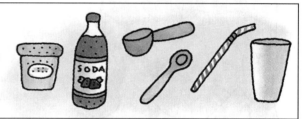

2. Pour strawberry soda over the ice cream.

3. Add a straw and a spoon. You're set!

Valentine Sundae

You Will Need

Vanilla ice cream   or   Strawberry ice cream
Strawberry topping   or   Marshmallow topping
Chocolate chips   or   Chocolate kisses
Maraschino cherry   or   Red sprinkles
Ice-cream scoop or spoon
Bowl

Steps

1. Put three scoops of ice cream in a bowl.

2. Pour a topping over the ice cream.

3. Scatter chocolate chips or kisses over the sundae.

4. Top with a cherry or red sprinkles.

5. Be creative! Use your imagination —
and your appetite — to create the best
valentine sundae of all.

Pin the Arrow on the Heart

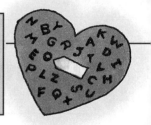

This is a new version of an old game that you can play with your friends on Valentine's Day. Instead of pinning a tail on a donkey, you pin an arrow on a heart full of initials. Whose initials will the arrow point to? That's when the fun begins.

Materials

Large piece of scrap paper or newspaper   Scissors
Large piece of red poster board (22"x 28")   Pencil
Black marker   Tape
Paper doilies (optional)   Handkerchief or scarf
Piece of yellow construction paper or poster board   Ruler

Steps

1. Make a pattern for a large heart on scrap paper or a sheet of newspaper. Fold the paper in half. Measure 12 inches for the width of one half of the heart. Measure 20 inches for the length of the heart. Cut out the pattern and unfold it.

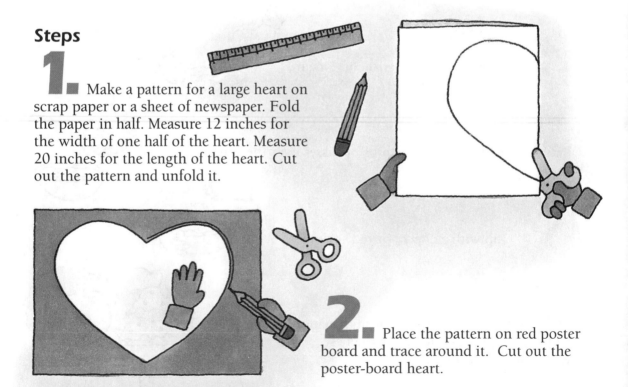

2. Place the pattern on red poster board and trace around it. Cut out the poster-board heart.

3. If you like, cut several paper doilies in half. Turn the heart over and tape the doilies to the edges of the heart, as shown.

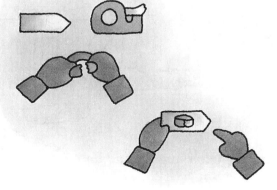

4. Write all the letters of the alphabet on the front of the heart with a pencil. Scatter the letters across the heart at random. Make thick capital letters. Then fill them in with a black marker.

5. Draw an arrow on yellow poster board or construction paper. Make it about one inch wide and four inches long. Cut out the arrow.

6. Cut a two-inch-long piece of tape and fasten the ends together, sticky side out. Press one side on the arrow; the other side will stick to the heart when the game is played.

continued...

7.

Fasten the heart to a wall with tape.

8.

Blindfold the first player with a scarf or handkerchief. Turn the player around several times and then point him or her, arrow in hand, in the direction of the heart. After the player pins the arrow on the heart, take off the blindfold and announce the letter to which it points.

9.

Everyone can try to guess whose name the letter might stand for. Check to see if the player's face is as red as the valentine heart!

Chocolate, Chocolate, Chocolate

Chocolate lovers love Valentine's Day! Here are some facts about the treat we love to eat:

♥ Chocolate is made from cacao beans, the seeds of the cacao tree. Cacao trees grow only in the tropics, near the equator. Cacao beans are grown in West Africa, the Indies, Mexico, and Central and South America.

♥ Many years ago, the word cacao was misspelled in English as cocoa. English-speaking countries began to call products of the cacao tree cocoa beans, cocoa butter, and cocoa powder.

♥ Cacao beans are harvested and processed into a thick liquid called chocolate liquor. This liquid is used to make all the delicious chocolate products we eat.

♥ Milk chocolate is the most popular of all chocolate products. Milk solids and sugar are added to chocolate liquor. The mixture is blended for over three days to make a smooth, sweet chocolate. Ninety percent of the chocolate consumed in the United States is milk chocolate.

♥ The Mayan and Aztec Indians of Central America and Mexico were the first to use chocolate. Spanish explorers brought cacao beans from Mexico to Spain in the 1500s. By the 1700s, chocolate and cocoa were popular throughout Europe. Today chocolate is a universal passion.

Chocolate Dips

The good things in life are even better when they're covered with chocolate — chocolate-covered peanuts, chocolate-covered marshmallows, or chocolate-covered strawberries. This recipe is for a chocolate sauce that you can use for dipping. Dip your favorite foods to make chocolate-covered Valentine's Day snacks.

You Will Need

16-ounce package of semisweet chocolate chips or pieces
4 tablespoons heavy cream
1/2 teaspoon vanilla
Food to dip (bananas, strawberries, cherries, apples, pretzels, marshmallows, nuts, cookies)
Double boiler

Large spoon
Measuring spoons
Wax paper
Potholder
Large dish or tray
Hot pad
Fork or kitchen tongs

Steps

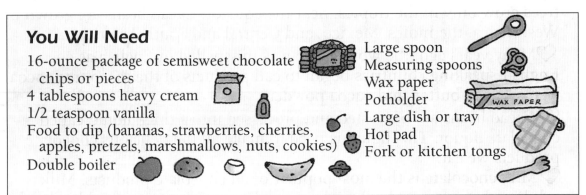

1. Prepare the fruits and other foods that you want to dip. They should be ready to use after you finish Step 5. Also have sheets of wax paper handy.

2. Put some water in the bottom of a double boiler, and heat the chocolate in the top section. Be careful not to let the chocolate burn. If you're not allowed to use the stove by yourself, ask an adult for help with this and the following steps.

3. Add the cream and vanilla to the melted chocolate.

4. Stir the mixture until it is uniformly smooth.

5. Turn off the stove. Use a potholder to take the top pan off the lower one. Set the pan on a hot pad on the kitchen table.

6. Use a fork or kitchen tongs to dip the food into the chocolate sauce. Cover each piece completely. Then set it on the wax paper to cool.

7. The chocolate will harden in 10 to 20 minutes. Place the treats on a serving dish. Your snacks are ready to eat!

Stupid Cupid Jokes

What does it mean when someone puts Xs at the bottom of a love letter?

Your sweetheart is double-crossing you.

How do vampires fall in love?

It's love at first bite.

What happens to love triangles?

They turn into wreck-tangles.

Which month has twenty-seven days?

All of them do

What flower is used most on Valentine's Day?

Tulips

Knock, knock.
Who's there?
Lemme.
Lemme who?
Lemme kiss you.

Knock, knock.
Who's there?
Ida.
Ida who?
Ida want to.

Knock, knock.
Who's there?
Olive.
Olive who?
Olive you.

A Hearty Mouse

Here's a mouse with a big heart made all of hearts. Use it as a decoration for a Valentine's party. Or write a secret message inside this squeaky sweetheart to give to your favorite person.

Materials

1 sheet gray construction paper
1 sheet pink construction paper
Tracing paper
Markers or crayons
Glue or tape
Shoelace licorice for tail

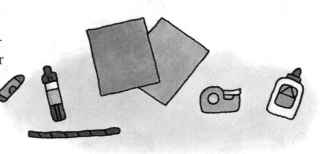

Steps

1A.

1. Using the pattern on page 22, trace the large heart onto the gray construction paper and cut out.

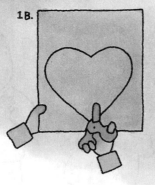
1B.

2A.

2B.

2. Fold the gray heart in half.

3. Using the small heart pattern on page 22, cut two small hearts out of the pink construction paper.

4. Glue or tape the pink heart ears on each side of the gray mouse.

5. Draw eyes and whiskers on your mouse with marker or crayon.

6. If you wish, unfold the mouse to write a message on the gray heart. Glue or tape the edges of the gray heart together to hold your mouse in place. Leave a small opening at the rounded end for its tail.

Be my Valentine

continued...

7. Insert your licorice tail.

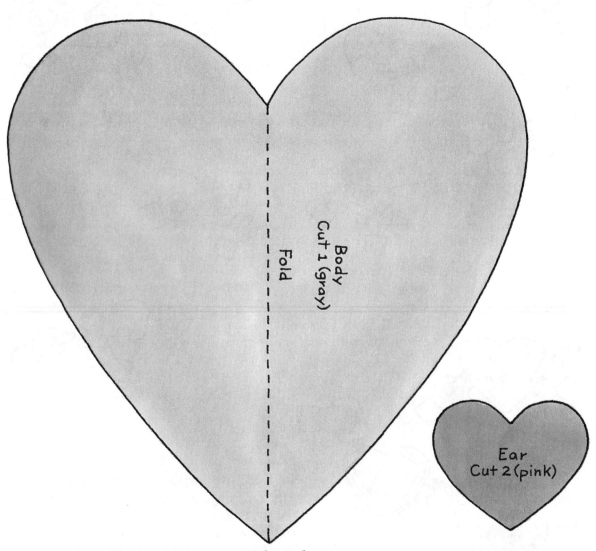

Body
Cut 1 (gray)

Fold

Ear
Cut 2 (pink)

Note: Use tracing paper to trace and cut these patterns.

Love Superstitions

Love is a mystery. Over the centuries, superstitions have arisen to explain that unexplainable feeling. Here are some favorite superstitions that have been around for many years. Try them — if you dare.

How can you make someone fall in love with you?

♥ Pull a hair from the head of the one you love.

♥ Make a love potion. Pick petals from red roses and white roses. Boil them in 365 drops of water for 3-$\frac{3}{4}$ minutes. Put 3 drops of the potion in your true love's drink.

23

continued...

How many people are in love with you?

♥ The answer is the number of times you can crack your knuckles.

Will you marry?

♥ The answer is yes if the lines in your palm form the letter M.
♥ The answer is no if you step on a cat's tail.

How can you predict to whom you will be married?

♥ Sleep with a mirror under your pillow, and you will dream of your future husband or wife.

Are you loved in return?

♥ Pluck the petals from a daisy. As you pull off each one, say "He/she loves me" or "He/she loves me not" alternately. What you say as you pull off the last petal tells you how your loved one feels about you.

Will you marry the one you love?

♥ Write your full name on a piece of paper. Write the name of the one you love underneath it. Cancel out identical letters in your two names. For example, cancel out one "a" in yours, then one "a" in his or hers. After finishing this, count the letters that remain in each name. As you count, say *friendship* after the first, *courtship* after the second, *marriage* after the third, *love* after the fourth, and *hate* after the fifth. Repeat in this order until no letters are left. Write down the word you said after the last letter in each name. This will predict how you will feel toward each other in the future.

　　Jennie Smith — marriage
　　Michael Jones — love

Heart Facts

♥ A valentine's heart is a symbol of love. But a real human heart is a strong, hard-working muscle that keeps you alive. Here are some amazing facts about your heart and what it does for you.

♥ Your heart is in the center of your chest, behind your breastbone. Its lower tip slants down to the left and is the only part you can feel beating. That's why your heart seems to be on the left side of your body.

♥ Your heart is about the size of your fist and weighs less than a pound.

♥ A child's heart beats about 90 times a minute. A baby's heart beats about 120 times a minute. An adult's heart beats about 60 to 80 times a minute.

♥ The heart is a powerful pump. When the heart muscles tighten and then relax, they force blood through the tubes of your circulatory system. This muscle movement is what you feel as your heartbeat.

♥ You have about three to four quarts of blood in your body. The heart pumps all this blood through your body in one minute. In other words, it takes only 60 seconds for a drop of blood to make a complete trip from your heart, through your body, and back again.

♥ An artery is a kind of tube that carries blood away from the heart. This is fresh blood containing oxygen from the lungs and dissolved food from the small intestine. A vein carries "used" blood back to the heart. This blood contains carbon dioxide and waste products. Millions of tiny blood vessels, called capillaries, connect arteries and veins. Our bodies have about 100,000 miles of arteries, veins, and capillaries.

♥ Your blood contains various cells, each with a special job to do. Red blood cells are shaped like saucers. Their job is to carry oxygen to the cells of your body. They also carry carbon dioxide back to your lungs. White blood cells are part of your body's defense system. They fight off disease and infection. Your blood also contains platelets. When you get a cut in your skin, platelets help form lumps or clots in the blood. This keeps the blood from flowing out of your body.

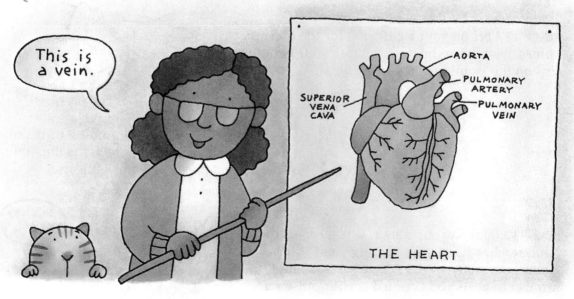

This is a vein.

AORTA

PULMONARY ARTERY

PULMONARY VEIN

SUPERIOR VENA CAVA

THE HEART

Heart-Throb Experiments

Measuring Your Heartbeat

You can feel your own heart beating by finding your pulse. A pulse is the bulging of an artery following each beat of the heart. Follow these steps to find your pulse and measure its rate.

You Will Need

Watch or clock with a second hand

Steps

1. Turn the inside of your right hand upward.

2. Use the first two fingers, not your thumb, of your left hand to find the pulse. (Your thumb has a pulse of its own.)

3. Feel on your right wrist for the bone that comes down from the thumb. Place your two fingertips on this point just below the wrist.

4. You should feel your pulse, or heartbeat, at this point. (If you don't, check the illustration for the correct position of your fingers.)

5. Look at your watch. When the second hand reaches 12, begin counting your heartbeats. Count until sixty seconds have passed. The number of beats you counted is your pulse rate.

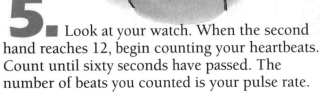

50, 51, 52 53, 54...

Exercise and the Heart

When you exercise, your muscles need more oxygen. The heart must beat faster to pump more oxygen-carrying blood to your muscles. A simple experiment shows how this affects your pulse rate.

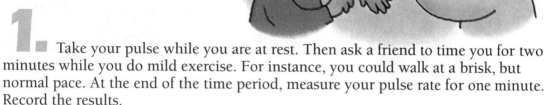

You Will Need

Watch or clock with a
    second hand
A friend

Steps

1. Take your pulse while you are at rest. Then ask a friend to time you for two minutes while you do mild exercise. For instance, you could walk at a brisk, but normal pace. At the end of the time period, measure your pulse rate for one minute. Record the results.

2. Ask your friend to time you for two minutes while you do heavy exercise. For instance, you could walk quickly or run. At the end of the time, measure your pulse rate for one minute. Record the results.

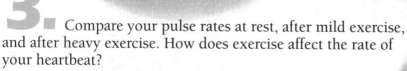

3. Compare your pulse rates at rest, after mild exercise, and after heavy exercise. How does exercise affect the rate of your heartbeat?

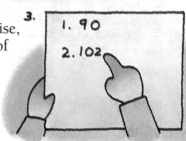

4. You should find that your pulse rate increases as the exercise you do becomes more strenuous.

29

Valentine Candy Box

Would you like to give someone a unique present for Valentine's Day? This candy box is easy to make and definitely one of a kind. It is made by using a decorating craft called decoupage. *Decoupage* (day-coo-PAHZH) means to decorate a surface with a collection of pictures, and then seal them with a clear finish. You can be as creative as you want with your decoupage! Add your valentine's initials or a message to make this gift special. When your candy box is finished, fill it with chocolates or other valentine treats.

Materials

Sturdy gift box or cigar box
Old magazines or valentine cards
Scissors
White glue

Paintbrush
Paper plate
Valentine candies

Steps

1. Find a box to use. A small gift box, like the kind jewelry comes in, works well. A cigar box is also ideal.

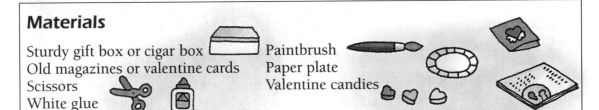

2. Look through old magazines or cards for valentine illustrations to cut out. Remember that this box can be as individual as you want. You can make it look as pretty or as humorous as you like.

3. If you'd like to add words or initials to the box, cut out the letters you need from magazines.

4. Arrange the pictures and letters on the lid of the box. Then, using white glue, secure them to the lid.

5. For the first step of the decoupage process, pour a small amount of white glue onto a paper plate. With a paintbrush, apply a thin layer of glue over the top of the box lid.

6. Let the glue dry. Add a second, a third, and a fourth layer of glue. Each time, let the glue dry before adding another layer.

7. The glue will dry into a shiny, hard surface. Your picture will look almost as though it has been painted on.

8. Fill the box with valentine candies and give it to someone special.

The Queen of Hearts

This Valentine's Day, work a little magic with the help of the Queen of Hearts. This famous card trick will amaze your friends. It seems like magic — until you know its secret.

You Will Need

Deck of cards
Table
A friend

Steps

1. To prepare for the trick, remove the Queen of Hearts from a deck of cards. Shuffle the cards well and place the Queen of Hearts on the bottom.

2. In front of a friend, spread out the deck of cards, face down. Ask him or her to pick one card, any card, from the deck. Ask your friend to look at the card, but not to let you see it.

3. Put the deck of cards on the table, face down, in a neat stack. Tell your friend to place his or her card on top.

4. Now "cut" the deck of cards. This means that you pick up the top half of the deck and put it down next to the rest of the deck. Then you pick up the bottom half and put it on top of the other pile. Cut the deck several more times. No matter how many times you cut the cards, the chosen card will always be under the Queen of Hearts.

5. Hold the deck of cards, face down, in your left hand. With your right hand, flip each card over, onto the table. Tell your friend that you will announce which card he or she chose when you see it. Keep flipping cards until you see the Queen of Hearts. The next card will be the one chosen by your friend!

The Lonely Queen

This is a card game that's fun to play on Valentine's Day. The rules are outlined below. You can add your own funny predictions for what might happen to the loser of the game.

How to Play

1. Use a regular deck of 52 playing cards. Remove the Queen of Hearts from the deck and set it aside.

2. One player is chosen as the dealer. The dealer deals out all the cards, one at a time, to each player.

3. The players pick up their cards and look through them for pairs. Each player takes the pairs from his or her hand and puts them on the table face down.

4. The player to the left of the dealer begins play by fanning out his or her cards, face down, and offering a choice of one card to the player to his or her left. It is important that the person choosing cannot see the faces of the cards.

5. The second player makes a choice and puts the card in his or her hand. If it makes a new pair, the player puts the pair down on the table. Next, this player fans out his or her cards, offers one to the player to the left, and the play continues around the table.

6. All players continue to select cards until they have nothing left in their hands. All the cards but one will have been put down in pairs. Since the Queen of Hearts was removed from the deck, there will be one Queen that will not have a match for a pair. Whoever ends up holding this single Queen is the loser of the game.

I lost...

Mysterious Messages

Would you like to send a valentine message to someone, but are shy about signing it? A secret code can come in handy on Valentine's Day for just such a thing! Or you can send a valentine with a mysterious message to someone you like. Here's how to do it.

This secret code substitutes the symbols shown below for the letters of the alphabet. Study it carefully. Then try to decode the message below it. (If you need help, the answer appears at the bottom of the page.)

The code

The message

The message is

Another kind of code is a jumbled-letter code. Reverse the order of the letters in each word and, instead of using a space between words, use a random letter, like X. Try to break this code.

Did you break the code? If not, see the answer below. Have fun sending mysterious messages on Valentine's Day!

Roses are red.
Violets are blue.
Romeo loved Juliet,
And I love you.

Valentines for Pets

Valentine's Day is for remembering the ones you love. If you have a pet, it may be very special to you. Show your dog, cat, fish, bird, hamster, or rabbit that you love it. Make it a Valentine's Day gift.

Doggie Cookies

This Valentine's Day, try a little home cooking for your dog. These biscuits are nutritious and tasty. See if your dog says, "Bow-wow!" for your cooking.

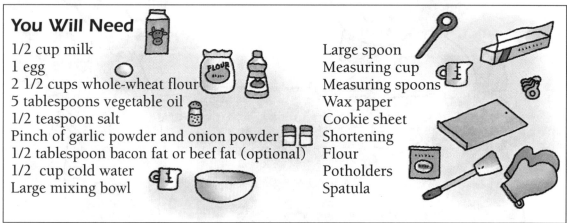

You Will Need

1/2 cup milk
1 egg
2 1/2 cups whole-wheat flour
5 tablespoons vegetable oil
1/2 teaspoon salt
Pinch of garlic powder and onion powder
1/2 tablespoon bacon fat or beef fat (optional)
1/2 cup cold water
Large mixing bowl

Large spoon
Measuring cup
Measuring spoons
Wax paper
Cookie sheet
Shortening
Flour
Potholders
Spatula

Steps

1. Preheat the oven to 350°F. If you're not allowed to use the oven by yourself, ask an adult for help.

2. Combine the milk, egg, vegetable oil, flour, salt, onion powder, and garlic powder in a large bowl. Stir well with a large spoon. If you like, add the bacon or beef fat for taste.

3. Add the cold water and continue stirring until a stiff dough forms.

4A.

FLOUR

4B.

4. Lay out a strip of wax paper on the table and sprinkle it with flour. Place the dough on the paper and flatten it with your hands until it is about half an inch thick.

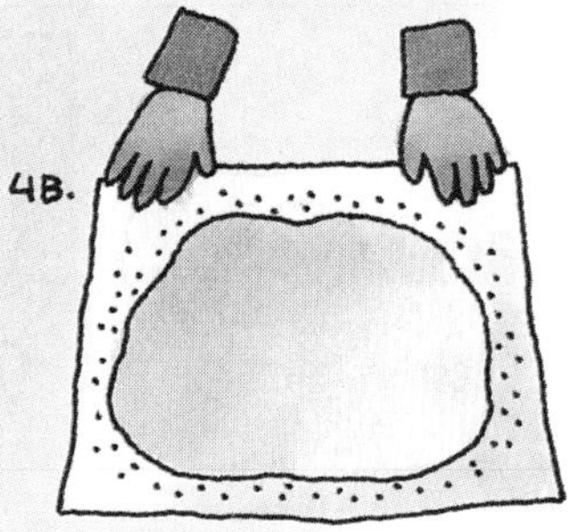

5. Divide the dough into 12 to 15 pieces. Roll the pieces of dough into balls.

6A.

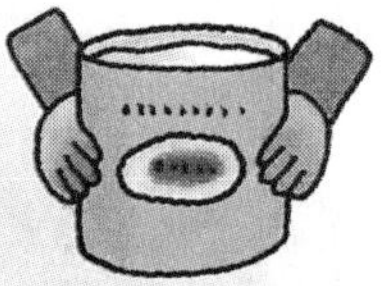

6. Ask an adult to help you grease a cookie sheet with shortening. Place the balls on the sheet and bake them in the oven for 35 minutes.

6B.

7. Using potholders and a spatula, remove the cookies from the sheet and let them cool. Give your dog two a day as a special treat.

A Catnip Heart

All cats love catnip. For Valentine's Day, you can make your cat a red heart stuffed with catnip.

Materials

Dried catnip (available at pet stores)
Red felt
Scissors

Needle and red thread
Heavy string

Steps

1. Cut out two identical hearts from red felt. They should measure approximately four inches across their widest part.

2. Lay one heart on top of the other and hold them together. Sew your seam about one quarter of an inch from the edge of the heart. Do not sew all the way around the heart; leave a small opening.

3. Fill the heart with catnip by stuffing it through the opening. Then stitch the opening shut.

4. Sew a loop of string or ribbon to the top of the heart.

5. Hang the heart from its ribbon so that it dangles for your cat to play with.

Hamster Toys

A few simple toys can add some fun to your hamster's life. And you'll be rewarded with many laughs, as you watch your pet at play.

You Will Need

4 ice-cream sticks   Glue
1/2-pint milk carton   Red marker
Scissors

Steps

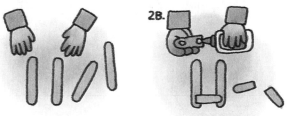

1. Wash and dry a small milk carton. Cut a hole in the side for the hamster to use as an entrance to its "clubhouse."

2. Arrange two ice-cream sticks about two inches apart. Break the other two sticks into pieces of two and one-half inches each. Glue the smaller pieces to the large sticks like the rungs of a ladder.

3. When the glue is dry, use a red marker to decorate the ladder with hearts.

4. Glue the ladder to the side of the milk carton.

5. Put the clubhouse and ladder into your hamster's cage. Wish your pet a Happy Valentine's Day!

Whatever your pet — a bird, fish, snake, guinea pig, rabbit, or turtle — think of something special you can do for it on Valentine's Day. Perhaps the best gift of all is a little extra attention and love.

Chocolate Fortune Cookies

These cookies make a great Valentine's Day surprise. Unlike regular fortune cookies, they are made with chocolate. And hidden inside them are funny fortunes. Bake a batch for your friends.

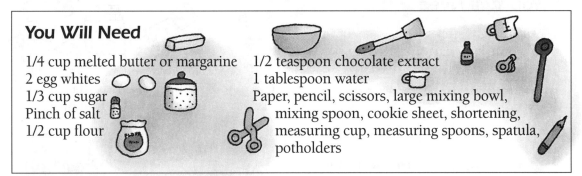

You Will Need

1/4 cup melted butter or margarine
2 egg whites
1/3 cup sugar
Pinch of salt
1/2 cup flour

1/2 teaspoon chocolate extract
1 tablespoon water
Paper, pencil, scissors, large mixing bowl,
    mixing spoon, cookie sheet, shortening,
    measuring cup, measuring spoons, spatula,
    potholders

Steps

1. Cut narrow pieces of paper, each about two inches long, for your fortunes. Write funny valentine predictions on them. For example: *You will marry a vampire; I'm kookie over you; Heartburn ahead.*

2. To begin cooking, combine the egg whites, salt, and sugar in a mixing bowl. Adding one ingredient at a time, stir in the flour, chocolate extract, melted butter, and water.

3. Put the mixture in the refrigerator to chill for 30 minutes. Meanwhile, preheat the oven to 350°F. (For this and other steps involving the oven, ask an adult for help.) Grease a cookie sheet with shortening.

4A.

4B.

4. Scoop out a rounded teaspoon of batter and drop it onto one end of the cookie sheet. Spread the batter into a circle (about three inches in diameter) with a spoon. Repeat for a second cookie at the other end of the sheet.

5. Bake the cookies for three to five minutes, or until the edges turn light brown. Using potholders, take the sheet from the oven.

5A.

5B.

6A.

6B.

6C.

6. Remove the cookies from the sheet with a spatula. Place them on a plate. Lay one of the fortunes in the middle of each cookie and quickly fold the round cookie in half. Push in the flat side of the semicircle to make a fortune-cookie shape.

7. Repeat Steps 4–6 for the rest of the batter. The recipe will make 20 to 24 fortune cookies.

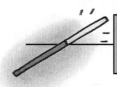

Valentine's Magic

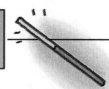

This trick is great for Valentine's Day because you make the color of the day, red, disappear. There is a scientific reason for the result — but to your audience, it looks like magic!

Materials

2 clear glasses Household bleach
Water Tablespoon
Red food coloring "Magic" wand (a chopstick or straw works well)

Steps

1A. 1B. 1C.

1. To prepare for the trick, fill one of the glasses with water. Carefully add two drops of red food coloring. Stir the mixture.

2.

2. Carefully measure two table-spoons of bleach into the second glass. The glass should still look empty to your audience.

3A. 3B.

3. Now you're ready to perform. Set the two glasses side by side on a table. Announce that you shall perform magic on the red water. Pour the red water from the first glass into the second glass. Stir the water into the bleach, using your magic wand.

4. Shout "Abracadabra!" as you bring your wand out of the water. The water will have turned clear!

Why It Happened

Household bleach contains a chemical called sodium hypo-chlorite. Water contains hydrogen and oxygen. When you mixed the water and bleach, the chlorine in the bleach combined with the hydrogen in the water. The oxygen left in the water combined with the red food coloring, forming a colorless compound. The same principle is at work when bleach is used to take stains out of laundry.

(Note: Be sure to throw away the water-and-bleach solution immediately. Wash the glasses very carefully before reusing.)

Trivia Quiz

1. One of William Shakespeare's most famous plays is named after two young lovers. What is the title of the play?

2. In *Alice in Wonderland*, who threatened to cut off Alice's head?

3. Who is Cupid? What does he have to do with Valentine's Day?

4. According to superstition, what does it mean if your shoelaces become untied?

5. What is leap year? When does it occur?

6. What flower is a symbol of love and is given most on Valentine's Day?

Answers to Trivia Quiz

1. *Romeo and Juliet* is the title. It is a play about a young man and woman who fall in love despite the fact that their families have long been enemies. The modern musical, *West Side Story,* is based on Shakespeare's play.

2. The Queen of Hearts is the cruel ruler who orders the servants to take off Alice's head.

3. Cupid was one of the gods worshiped by the ancient Romans. His mother, Venus, was the goddess of love and beauty. Cupid himself was a very handsome young man who carried a quiver full of gold-tipped arrows. His favorite sport was to shoot his arrows into the hearts of humans and the gods. Anyone shot with one of Cupid's arrows would immediately fall in love.

    Today, Cupid is a symbol of love. Many valentine hearts still have an arrow through them, a reminder of Cupid's power.

4. The superstition is that if your shoes become untied, it's because the one you love is thinking of you.

5. Leap year arrives every fourth year when an extra day is added to the calendar. That day is February 29. Leap year makes up for the difference between our usual calendar year, and the actual time it takes Earth to revolve around the sun, which is 365-$\frac{1}{4}$ days each year.

6. The rose stands for love and is the most popular Valentine's Day flower.

Happy Valentine's Day

48